WILD HORSES

Poems by
KENNETH STEVEN

Illustrations by
JOHN BUSBY

SAINT ANDREW PRESS

First published in 2002 by
SAINT ANDREW PRESS
121 George Street
Edinburgh EH2 4YN

ISBN 0 7152 0798 9

British Library Cataloguing in Publication Data
A catalogue record for this book is available from the British Library

Published with grant assistance from the
Drummond Trust, 3 Pitt Terrace, Stirling

Typeset in Ellington by Waverley Typesetters, Galashiels
Printed and bound in the United Kingdom by The Cromwell Press, Wiltshire

CONTENTS

ISLAND ❧ 1

RIVER ❧ 3

THE CATHEDRAL ❧ 5

THE BIRTH OF THE FOAL ❧ 7

HIGHLAND BULL ❧ 8

MEETING ❧ 9

TORTOISESHELL ❧ 11

GATHERING SLOES ❧ 13

CURLEWS ❧ 15

THE PHOTOGRAPHS ❧ 17

STILL ❧ 19

DONALD ❧ 20

MOLE ❧ 21

THE WINDOW ❧ 23

THE CALVINIST ❧ 24

DINGLE ❧ 25

THE WIND AND MOON ❧ 27

VOICES ❧ 29

KITTENS ❧ 31

ELLEN'S MOON ❧ 33

PLOUGHING MATCH ❧ 35

THE BAT ❧ 36

BALRANALD ❧ 37

DRAGONFLIES ❧ 38

SEA URCHINS ❧ 39

THE DEER ❧ 40

CARSEBRECK ❧ 41

THISTLES ❧ 43

THE SHEEPDOG ❧ 45

WILD GOOSE CHASE ❧ 47

THE CORNCRAKE ❧ 49

LISTENING ❧ 51

BRAMBLES ❧ 53

BEES ❧ 54

TRAVELLERS ❧ 55

THE KINGFISHER ❧ 57

GREY GEESE ❧ 59

ELEVENTH NOVEMBER ❧ 60

TRUST ❧ 61

REMEMBER ❧ 63

ACKNOWLEDGEMENTS ❧ 64

To the memory of Bill Leadbetter
Art teacher and friend

ISLAND

I remember what it was like to barefoot that house,
Wood rooms bleached by light. Days were new voyages,
    journeys,
Coming home a pouring out of stories and of starfish.
The sun never died completely in the night,
The skies just turned luminous, the wind
Tugged at the strings in the grass like a hand
In a harp. I did not sleep, too glad to listen by a window
To the sorrow sounds of the birds
As they swept down in skeins, and rose again, celebrating
All that was summer. I did not sleep, the weight of school
Behind and before too great to waste a grain of this.
One four in the morning at first larksong I went west over the
    dunes,
Broke down running onto three miles of white shell sand, and
    stood.
A wave curled and silked the shore in a single seamless breath.
I went naked into the water, ran deep into a green
Through which I was translucent. I rejoiced
In something I could not name; I celebrated a wonder
Too huge to hold. I trailed home, slow and golden,
Dried by the sunlight.

RIVER

Three days and nights it rained
Fingertips on windows, a stammering
On corrugated iron roofs. The lion colours
Of September drained
To leave an ancient face – pale and gaunt, eyes glazed –
Embedded in the land.

At night quite suddenly, the rain went dead.
A loud silence rang in my ears;
I looked out, listened,
Heard only the huge hall of the river
Breathing downstream.

I went to stand in the roaring darkness
As the river silvered past
With chinks of moonlight.
The gored groins of the hills
In its hands, in these hundred thousand hands –
A myriad magicians –
All the long curl
The turn and fall
Into the sea.

When they came first to this land
In the beginning
They beat through the many greens of the woods
To this endless water –
Soft syllables sifting and searching,
Revelling in their own language.

These were the first words they made:
Tamar, Lyon, Shannon, Earn and Evelix –
These were the stirrings of the kingdom
The oldest human bones that are,
The boulder stones of all we know.

THE CATHEDRAL

When lights lemon the river in June
And the river is so low a boy could plash across,
Barbecues glow along the banks, their meat
Dribbling and crackling. If you go upstream –
The dusk sky blue, the clearest liquid blue –
If you go barefoot as far as the cathedral,
You will see the bats tipping and flitting the water
Like pieces of muslin, the air rank with their scent.
Their wings click as they turn, as they nip midges,
Softly weaving patterns through the trees
Till milky, stars come out, and it is dark at last.

THE BIRTH OF THE FOAL

My eyes still fought with sleep. Out over the fields
Mist lay in grey folds, from vague somewheres
Curlews rose up with thin trails of crying. Our lanterns
Rocked in soft globes of yellow, our feet
Slushed through the early morning thickness of the grass.

She lay on her side, exhausted by her long night;
The hot smell of flanks and head and breath
Ghosted from her spread length.
Sunlight cracked from the broken yolk of the skies,
Ruptured the hills, spangled our eyes and blinded us,
Flooded the pale glows of our lanterns.

There he lay in a pool of his own wetness:
Four long spindles scrabbling, the bigness of his head, a bag of a
    body –
All struggling to find one another, to join up, to glue
Into the single flow of a birthright. He fought
For the first air of his life, noised like a child.

His mother, still raw and torn from the scar of his birth,
Turned, and her eyes held him,
The great harsh softness of her tongue stilled his struggle.

We knelt in the wet grass, dumbed
By a miracle, by something bigger than the sun.

HIGHLAND BULL

He is just an ornament on the moorland
Made of heather roots, too tough for meat;
A piece of old machinery with handlebars
Left out to rust in all weather.

Americans will stop their cars
In a force ten August, iron rain –
Looking for the bull's front end
And a snatched picture.

Yet in him somewhere is an engine room
Quite capable of firing.
Tickle the bracken beast
With care, with a little Gaelic.

MEETING

Today I met a journeyman thatcher.
He had not been born with that life in his blood;
One day he just dug up his roots and left,
Never looked back.

He said that sometimes as he swept the thatch
Up onto a roof and heard the shingle of the trees,
The fields' chase, he was blown
Out of the mad motorway of this age

To a place that you never could buy,
A place that is on no map.
He had heard it and touched it in roofs,
In thatch, just once or twice, for a moment.

In him now the back lanes, the side roads
Of a timeless time, a land where hay ricks
Still jolt and topple. I sensed the sunlight in him
Warm as a whole summer.

TORTOISESHELL

Out of the blue
On the edge of a gust of sunlight
A thing no bigger than a leaf.

It opened like a book
The brown covers of its wings
And inside I saw

The embroidered golds and oranges and blues
Of an emperor's fabled chambers –
Each lattice window finished, painted perfect.

To think this thing
No stronger than a breath,
No bigger than a single tear of paper

Had slept all winter
Hidden in some edge of dark
For this brief flurry of days

(Such little time
To learn to fly,
To dance the skies)

Only to be blown away
Like a leaf
With the first whiff of autumn.

GATHERING SLOES

After the first frost
The land is jagged;
The hills are cut like broken glass,
Their tips sharp with snow.

I march along the farm track,
Hands swollen huge and red,
My feet squeaking on ice,
Breath dragoning the air.

I have come for the sloes –
Berries the colour of bruises –
Besieged by thorns, by sharp spears
That jab and tingle, draw little beads of blood.

In the kitchen's cool, dark hold
The sloes are gored one by one
By a skewer, then sunk in a half bottle of gin
That is left to sleep high on a scullery shelf.

Every day the bottle is turned
Till Christmas. The finished liquid is red,
Full of all the ripeness of the hedgerows –
The blood of autumn.

CURLEWS

Down at the river and always far away
I hear them, high voices crying,
The sky over that way blue and pale as opals.
Until it is dark I hear them mourning
Like lovers leaving for another land,
Circling over the summer river pools
The sea in their wings now, in their voices,
As they rise, restless, still cry and cry,
Till the first white stars have flowed like pearls
Through the water of the skies.

THE PHOTOGRAPHS

Downstairs she stands in the early morning light
Trying not to think of her son in London
Who does not come home any more.
The hills are hunched and terrible
Under bulls of late September cloud;
Outside the wind drags its fingers over the field,
The sea is ploughed, sharp bits of rain
Crystal against the window.
She must feed the hens, mend the fence,
Cut the wood, set the fire ... But first
She twists the radio, thumbs the dial
Through forecasts, German, crackling and an English voice,
To the sudden clear heart of a waltz.
She cannot turn it off, she stands again in the window
As a sudden blade of sun ruptures the hills,
Bloods them with priceless light. Now
She remembers her husband turning to her,
The shy curl of his smile, the dance of his eyes,
Their young son on his shoulders, chattering
Excited rubbish. These are the photographs
With the tattered edges
She keeps – these are all she has left.

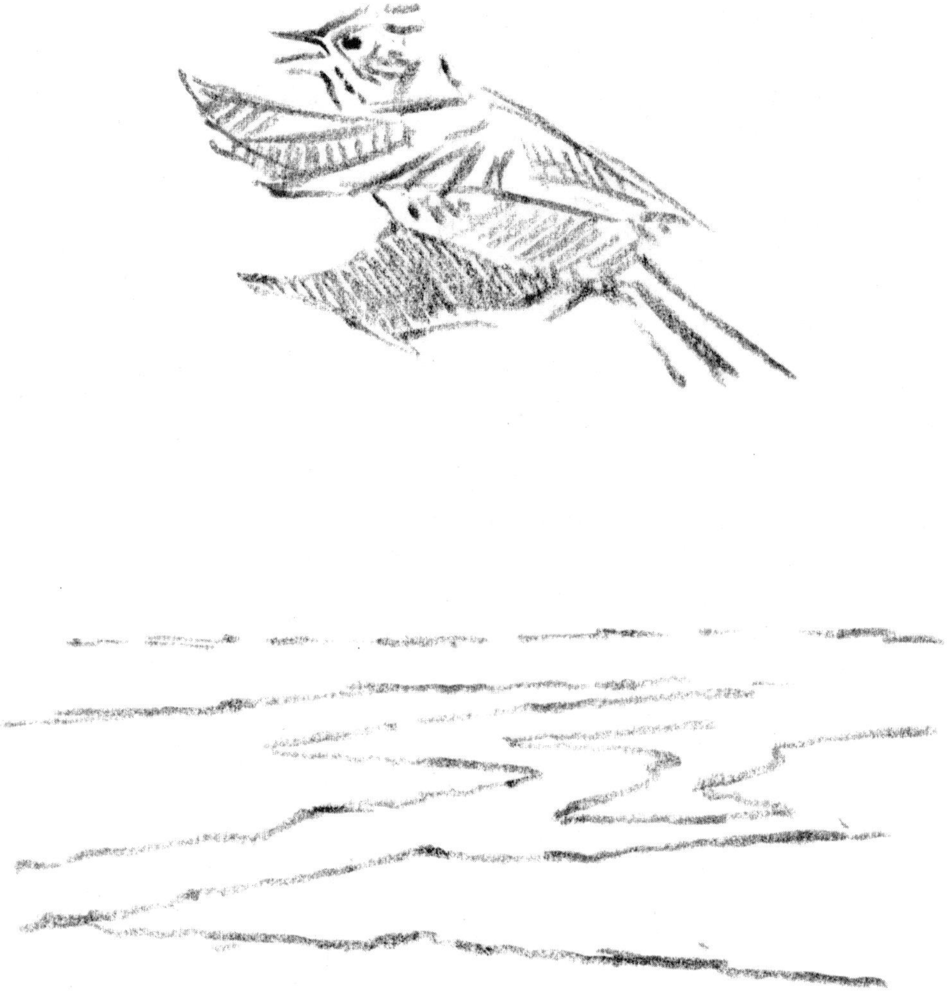

STILL

beside the little chefs and the burger kings
the constant thrumming of engines in the lanes
that burn north and south to housing estates
that look the same in merseyside and melbourne

off the motorways and the dual carriageways
take a first left and then a right, drive on
down the bump and turning of a track you never knew
then thud the car door shut and stand and listen

the thin gracenotes of a lark twirling in a may sky
above the open saltmarsh and the early morning light
the sea's white kettledrums beyond, the burnished sun
goldening a whole deep field of buttercups and grass

DONALD

I see him sitting there
His hills in the favourite window
Where lambing has come these seventy years
Easily to his hands. In the ploughed fields
That make up this face are crops of stories,
Whole ears of listening: tales of foxes,
The bad throats of ravens, strange fires
Guttering without reason on a barren moor.
He has written them across the pages of his mind
And in his eyes their key still winks a little gold,
Until the day he closes, and the manuscripts,
Illumined with primrose and amethyst,
Are buried in his field for ever.

MOLE

Paddling about on the path
Like a grandfather looking for his spectacles
He snuffled through last year's leaves
And with wide pink hands flung out
Sudden clumps of earth, his head
Evicting worms. That huge one came –
Eight inches of writhing anger
In Celtic knots on the ground.
Slowly, using both hands, the mole ate dinner
There on the spread table of the daylight.

THE WINDOW

The water coming in among the stone toes of the Hebrides,
Atlantic water, somewhere between green and blue,
Light like a gem.

All afternoon we plashed ankle-deep through low tide;
Crabs climbed carefully across a white silence,
Flounders boomed away in puffs of sand.

And far away, out towards Ireland,
Gannets drummed into the sea, plume on plume,
Deep into a shoal of herring.

And I was laughing all the time,
Scuffing water with my feet and laughing,
In the stained glass window of the summer.

THE CALVINIST

The heron is a Presbyterian minister
Standing gloomy in his long grey coat
Looking at his own reflection in a Sabbath loch.

Every now and again, pronouncing fire and brimstone,
He snatches at an unsuspecting trout
And stands with a lump in his throat.

The congregation of midges laughs at him in Gaelic;
He only prays for them, head bent into grey rain,
As a lark sings psalms half a mile above.

DINGLE

An Irish girl with hair like bracken
Rusting in autumn, and a voice of soft water,
Told of a place she found where dolphins come
Up out of sea the colour of an old wolf,
And there is nothing left between there and America.

I am not sure
It if was the truth, or just a story
Mingled with whisky, but it was beautiful,
And I put it in my pocket like a pebble
To keep and polish.

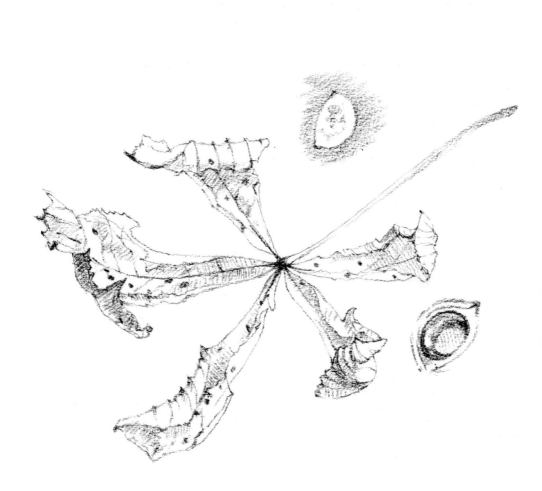

THE WIND AND THE MOON

The wind woke me, the loud howl of it
Boomed round the house and I felt at sea;
I fastened my eyes and was out in a ship,
Ten miles of Atlantic. I went to the window,
Watched the whole round of the moon
Ploughing through clouds, a coin
Of silver and gold.

All night I was blown between dreams,
Never slept deep, was thinking
Of the trees crashing and rising with wind,
Of the chestnut rain that would fall
By the morning.

At dawn I woke up, went out
Into the bright blue whirl of the wind,
Rode the wild horse of it upwards
Into the wood and beyond,
To the hill with the chestnut trees,
The leaves dancing at my feet
Russet and gold.

I ran and ran till my chest
Hurt with my heart. Under the hands of the chestnuts
That waved and swung in the air,
Saddles of leather, polished and shining,
Broken from the beds of their shells –
A whole hoard.

I went home in a gust of light
My pockets and hands
Knobbled with conkers.

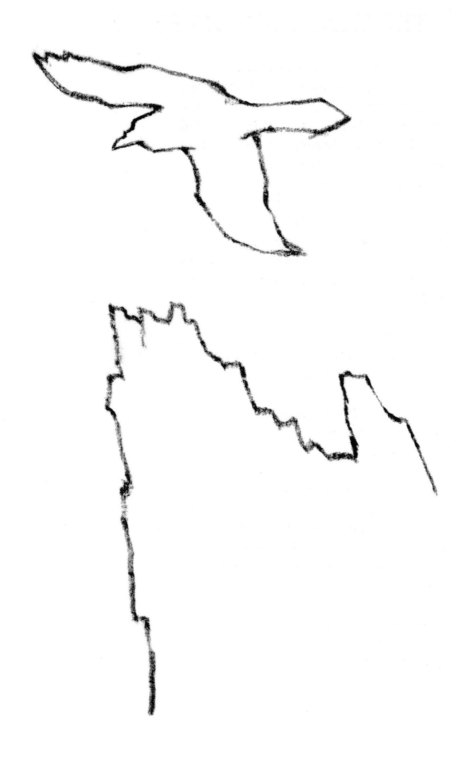

VOICES

The woodpecker taps out Morse,
Crows scrawl arguing across dawn in German.

Woodpigeons make soft French love words
As little twigs of sparrows chatter in Italian.

The raven is Norse, his voice chipped from sharp cliffs,
And geese squabble over Icelandic sagas.

In the middle of winter all I can hear are the curlews,
Crying at night their Gaelic laments.

KITTENS

In the dark of the shed the tractor slept
Like a Cyclops. Outside, spring fields lay dazed in light,
The hills were tugged by gusts of sleet.

I closed the door and listened. Nothing.
Then I heard the smallest sound, a searching,
Over there at the back of the darkness.

I crept closer, bent, found them –
A tangle of mewing and trembling –
Three rickety bags of milk and a mother,

Their eyes nothing more than cuts
In the dung-dark of the shed. I knelt and lifted them,
Black scraps of softness,

Their purrs throbbing their ribs,
Louder even than the snow wind
Snarling the door.

Born at the beginning of the year
In the banging cold of March
On the edge of the Highlands;

Unwanted things that would limp
From winter to winter by mice,
And the odd kindness of a farmer's wife.

ELLEN'S MOON

After we had gone
Through the heavy scent of the garden

Where apples and pears
Were just softening with redness

All the sky was shadowed
Mauve like the wings of pigeons

And you caught sight of the moon
Through the broken wall

Lifting from the battlements of cloud
Away to the distant south.

We laboured the hillside to see it
To get above those trees, and as we turned

And turned again, it was there, bonfiring them,
Splinters of amber and broken gold in the branches,

Until at last, high, it ballooned huge and clear
Over the fields in their white harvest seas

Where the tractors were clearing their throats cantankerously,
Bales being arranged in their places

Like reluctant schoolchildren. But the quiet grew and grew,
Every second the blue bigger, the night huger,

And the globe of the moon
Milk-white, swimming over everything, a strange magic.

PLOUGHING MATCH

October 17th. The chestnut trees are flinted and alight,
The skies are made of ice. But in this field
Under the low hill rims
Tractors ramble round like great red beetles, smoking.

Men stand in little knots, all wide red smiles
And talk of town and cattle feed and Christmas,
While their women folk, wrapped up like hens,
Sip tea and whisper to the collies by their feet.

Then the Clydesdales clamber into place. They jingle
With a jewellery of harnesses and ancient things
Kept bright on every farm. The plough blades bite the earth –
Green fields fold over black; the lines go straight as stakes.

And suddenly it is not now but then –
A hundred years and more ago, and every one of us
Knows horse scents, horse names, horse secrets, stories –
The roads are paved with grass.

And tonight the ploughmen who have proved their hands and
 eyes
Will dance away the dark in barns that reel with tunes;
And if their luck is lit, they'll blush the cheeks
Of girls who burned their hearts through every furrow.

THE BAT

It smelled of muslin, dank and dark,
This fallen newborn lying in the crystals
Of an early morning dew.

The size of my child's thumb;
Wings in segments that folded in on one another,
Tight beads of eyes.

In it were all the myths and legends
That had flown into the six years
Of my lying awake in the night.

But when I held it I was not afraid;
It was made of such soft intricacy
That I smoothed the fur of its head,

Whispered a prayer
As I slipped it into a grave
No larger than a snowdrop.

BALRANALD

This place on the edge of living
Shut in by the gales and the whipped water
Broken like sweet cream on the toothless rocks.
Here the birds shuffle along the sand on tiptoe,
Rise with weeping into a mouth of wind
And the gulls scream like Viking raiders.
There, out on the last of the eye's journey,
Sun coins a golden headland, the sky lights blue,
And suddenly the day is made of summer.
Who can translate the curlew's sadness
Into late evening across the moor –
A voice as precious as psalms.

DRAGONFLIES

The first time I saw them I was only ten;
I had struggled half an hour through heather
To the round brooch of that hill loch.
It was June, sunlight hot on every stone and hollow;
I wanted home to the dark cool of the corridors,
A hiding place and a book.
Then all at once I saw the dragonflies, like silent helicopters,
Their gauze wings thin and brittle
As the windows of a Chinese lantern.
Low they steered over pools and reed beds,
The blue of their bodies bold
As the splash on a kingfisher's breast.
But when suddenly I got up, mad to catch one,
Lumbered clumsily and loudly over boulders,
They vanished in a breath, soft as the breeze,
Drifted into the distance like blue thread.

SEA URCHINS

At the luminous edges of the Hebrides
Where silk water harps the shore
And the beaches are huge boomerangs
Necklaced with seaweed – they appear sometimes, curved things
Sharp as hedgehogs, their plates rose
And gold, or even the same green
As Venus at first light. Often
Crusts of waves crack them to pieces
Leave them in jewelled brooches
Up high beside grass and larks.
But each boy dreams of the morning
He looks down on the beach and catches
There at the lips of the water
One unbroken ball rolled
Out of the hand of the sea.

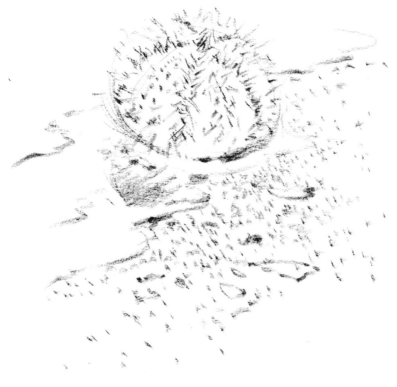

THE DEER

Come December they click at nightfall,
When the hills are ghostly with snow,
Flint-hoofed into a town iced by moonlight.

They are whittled from wood;
Sinews of strength sewn together,
Their hearing honed to catch the slightest falls in the forest
Or know the click of a gun.

Their mouths soften the grass of gardens
Before dogs nose them, bound out barking, big-voiced,
Send them no louder than a scattering of leaves
Back into the huge night.

CARSEBRECK

We drummed the car doors shut and stood
Looking over a place under bluest water.

A sudden curlew rose up crying,
Dripping a necklace of broken pearls.

We pushed through pools that lipped our ankles,
As the swans flowed over their flooded land.

A reed bunting nodded on a flute of grass,
Was blown away by a bit of breeze.

The geese came scrawling in from nowhere,
Skidded on water and squabbled over grass.

And the sun rose jagged from the world's rim,
Drenched us in soft and orange fire.

THISTLES

Like Pictish warriors, thick-skinned
Armed to the teeth with daggers
They sway whispering on the hill's crown.

After losing the battle of autumn
The amethyst bonnets fray
Their weapons start to rust.

The seed of their children
Balloons away on the wind's edge
Lighter than the feather of a wren.

THE SHEEPDOG

The sheepdog is all bounce –
A stream of black and white,
Eyes the colour of the Atlantic,
His bark a gun, jumping
Poacher and fox.

With the shepherd he is an endless flowing,
Waterfalling the field, eyes carved to one unblinking stare,
Able to flatten into nothing on command,
Become a pelt buried in the grass
Till the sheep are huddled like quartz boulders –
One single knot.

Inside the farm at night he lies dead,
Eyes like glass, the planed head
Stretched to the edge of the fire.

WILD GOOSE CHASE

Under a bridge
Something like a print.

A paw, perhaps, passed by
At midnight, padding

North, and leaving
Just a hint of fish.

Trail all day
Catch glimpses, ripples

That could be
Might be

A piece of otter
Playing Houdini

Melted into water
Gone to ground.

THE CORNCRAKE

Lying awake on Hebridean nights, too warm,
The sky made of opals, liquid blue and lemon,
The sea a faint white line of chalk
Hushing the shore – you heard the corncrake,
Like scissors scraping on stone, a metallic grating,
Hour after hour as the warm wind breathed
Through the open window and you wanted to sleep,
You wanted to chase that bird away,
Till suddenly you stopped and thought
How all December you would remember this
In the middle of the town's dark slush
And want back, to the curlews and the orchids,
And even the sleepless calling of the corncrake.

LISTENING

That evening, the seaplane nodded on a hidden edge of river.
First, the two boys clambered in the back,
Scrapping like young bears.
We followed, folded in behind the dials, knees in our chests.
Lars steered out, hammered the plane across the water,
Till suddenly we rose, and all of Finnmark fell away,
The sun climbed diamond from a ledge of sky
To light a hundred lakes. Reindeer battled out beneath,
Streaming from the aircraft's sudden coming;
Our shadow passed across the hills –
A slow midge drifting south.

We came down on the tundra –
A white curve against the wind –
A thousand feet up, forty miles from any road.
All around the cabin nets and paddles, drums of oil, old wood,
Then nothing, only lake and moor and lake.

I listened, waiting for the silence, and heard instead,
A sky full of voices –
Great northern divers, phalaropes, curlews, grebes –
An ancient chorus sung
Since the beginning.

BRAMBLES

A sky scudding overhead,
Huge and shaking with wind,
With the great restless searching of autumn.
The fields tawny, rustling like lions,
The hedgerows thick and dark with brambles.
I picked them – shiny, black, polished beads –
Till my hands were red and sore,
Till it was time to go and I knew
A whole year would whirl away
Before I came back there
Like a child, for brambles.

And why do I need this,
Why does it burn in me each September,
The yearning to go into the blow of the wind
To pick fruit till my fingers bleed?
Is it my grandfather and his before him
Still alive in my hands, somewhere,
Remembering autumn, remembering the beautiful pain
Of being alive?

BEES

In winter, when the days sting white with cold,
And all the hills are glazed,
We forget them.

Then one day, without a warning,
As if the earth has tilted into light,
The birds awaken and the land is gold.

Till out of nowhere the bees hum tawny,
Drizzle through the flowers, motorway the air,
Rumble through the insides of our windows.

They are like the drones of bagpipes,
Furry things that carry in their wings
A thousand flights of pollen.

Strange that all their lives
Should be homogenized, a weight of journeys
Made sweet and pure as honey.

TRAVELLERS

When the women came to the door
You could always tell who they were.
Something in the hair, the eyes,
That hadn't settled, that was not mortgaged
To a town. They carried baskets,
Clothes, toys – poor things for a few pence.

My mother asked them in,
Gave them broth on wild, November days
That blustered wind and rain about the house.
She never sent them off without some gift;
They thanked her with their smoky voices, rough,
And as I watched them I thought they looked like horses,
Unbroken horses that didn't fear the fields,
That could sleep easy in the lee of hills,
Ride from stable to stable,
Rough-shod.

Their men met them on the corners,
Red with drink. They disappeared, all of them together,
Like autumn leaves.

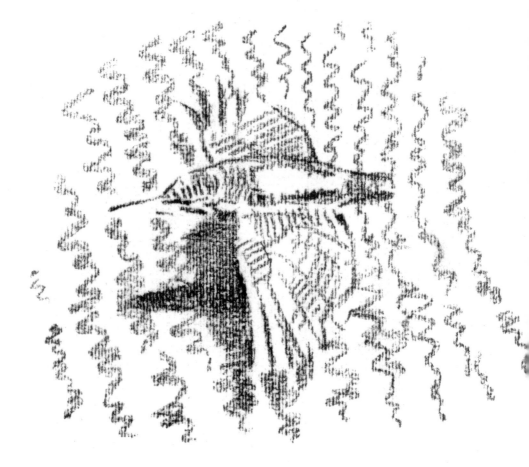

THE KINGFISHER

One early May we went there, on foot,
Through the ghostly cobwebs of the morning,
Hearing the curlews rising in hauntings across the fields.
The land was muddy, a guttural rushing of syllables
After long spring rain, so our boots were sucked and glutted
By a swilling of mire. We struggled though screens of trees,
Nets of rain meshing our faces, till we broke out
By that little trickle of stream –
Nothing more than a slither of thick water
Rippling away in different shades of inks.

Then, from nowhere, that blue bolt came
Bright as a dragonfly, a bit of summer sky,
Low as some skiffed stone, threading the reeds
To catch a branch, to lock
Into the sapphire thrill of kingfisher.
We stood amazed, gazing, ages,
Unable to believe the piece of luck we'd stumbled on.
We have kept that blue ever since
Somewhere in the winter attics of our world –
A priceless place, a whole kingdom.

GREY GEESE

All night they flew over in skeins.
I heard their wrangling far away,
Went out to look for them long after midnight,
Saw them silvered by the moonlight, like waves,
Flagging south, jagged and tired,
Across the sleeping farms and the autumn rivers
To the late fields of autumn.

Even in a city I have heard them,
Their noise like the rusty wheel of a bicycle;
I have looked up from among the drum of engines
To find them in the sky,
A broken arrowhead turning south,
Heading for home.

The Iceland summer, the long light,
Has run like rivers through their wings,
Strengthened the sinews of their flight
Over the whole ocean, till at last they circle,
Straggle down on the chosen runway of their field.

They come back
To the same place, the same day, without fail;
Precision instruments, a compass
Somewhere deep in their souls.

ELEVENTH NOVEMBER

That November morning
It had not dawned, dark
Was heavy on the trees
Velveting the road.

The car furred into the distance,
Lights opening in wool whiteness
Corners, bringing flickers of tree and hill
Out of them, moments of sharpness.

Like that I caught the fox
Curled in prayer;
Gloved by the shadows,
The blink of a picture –

The red beneath his head
Where the car had banged
To break his run, his breath –
Leave him on the hard shoulder,

A question, cold and still.
But all that dawn, that day,
Was changed – echoed, remembered –
The world was a fox smaller.

TRUST

Five days the snow had lain
Deep as a boot. Mouths of ice
Hung from roofs and windows,
The river slid by like a wolf.

At noon I went out with crumbs
Cupped in one hand. As I crouched,
A robin fluttered from nowhere,
Grasped the landfall of my palm.

A rowan eye inspected me
Side on. The blood-red throat
Swelled and sank, breathing quickly,
Till hungry, the beak stabbed fast.

The robin finished, turned,
Let out one jewel of sound,
Then ruffled up into the sky –
A skate on the frosty air.

REMEMBER

There will be only a few days like this –
The low sun flinting the house
Through the green sea of the trees as you stand
Struck, blessed, bathed in the same light
That rose life once from the young earth, that appled
The first child's cheeks.
There will be only a few days like this
To stop doing and stand, blinking,
As the leverets tumble in the bright field
And a cuckoo's moss voice calls from a far wood.
Wait until the sun has gone in broken orange
Down beneath the hills, and the blue sky
Hurts with the sudden shudder of the dusk.
Give thanks and turn and go back home –
For there will be only a few days like this.

Poems in *Wild Horses* have appeared in the following journals:

The Herald (Glasgow), *The Scots Magazine, The Countryman, Queen's Quarterly* (Canada), *The Yorkshire Journal, Poetry Scotland, The Sydney Morning Herald* (Australia), *The Poet's Voice,* TES *Primary, Westerly* (Australia), *New Welsh Review, Planet, Skinklin Star, Northwords, Staple, Moonstone, The New Writer, Atlanta Review* (US), *Envoi, Salt* (Australia), *The Month, The North, The New Quarterly* (Canada), *University of Windsor Journal* (Canada), *Poetry Review, Redoubt* (Australia), *Famous Reporter* (Australia), *and Chapman.*